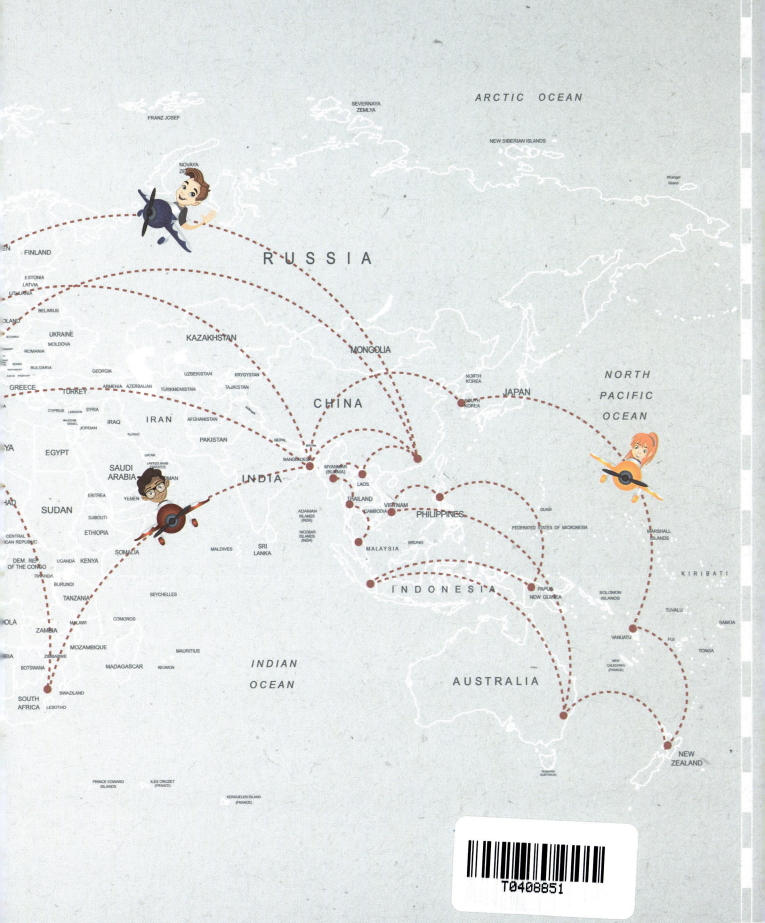

First Published 2022 by
Redback Publishing
PO Box 357 Frenchs Forest NSW 2086
Australia

www.redbackpublishing.com
orders@redbackpublishing.com

ISBN 978-1-922322-35-7 HBK

Author: Jane Hinchey
Editor: Caroline Thomas
Design: Redback Publishing

Original illustrations © Redback Publishing 2022
Originated by Redback Publishing

Printed and bound in Malaysia

Acknowledgements
Abbreviations: l—left, r—right, b—bottom, t—top, c—centre, m—middle
We would like to thank the following for permission to reproduce photographs:
(Images © shutterstock, wikimediacommons)
p7mr puwanai, p10br joloei, p11tr rotsukhon lam, p11bl Sophon Nawit,
p12bl Bundesarchiv, B 145 Bild-F009754-0005 / CC-BY-SA 3.0, CC BY-SA 3.0 DE
(https://creativecommons.org/licenses/by-sa/3.0/de/deed.en), p15bl Jack PhotoWarp,
p16tl isarescheewin, p18tl Bangprikphoto, p18bl Wanchana Phuangwan, p24tr think4photop,
p25tl Youkonton, p25tr Patryk Kosmider, p25mr Gina Smith, p28br Guimet Museum,
Public domain, via Wikimedia Commons (https://upload.wikimedia.org/wikipedia/
commons/4/4b/Petite_jarre_Mus%C3%A9e_Guimet_2418.jpg),

Disclaimer
Every effort has been made to contact copyright holders of any material reproduced in this book.
Any omissions will be rectified in subsequent printings if notice is given to the publisher.

A catalogue record for this
book is available from the
National Library of Australia

CONTENTS

Map of Thailand 4

Welcome to Thailand 6

Top Sites 8

Daily Life 10

Education 11

National Dress 12

Language 13

Life in Cities 14

Life in Rural Areas 15

Religion 16

A Land of Temples 18

Food 20

Landscape 22

Geography and Climate 24

Fabulous Flora and Fauna 26

The Arts 28

Flags, Symbols and Emblems 30

Glossary 31

Index 32

MAP OF THAILAND

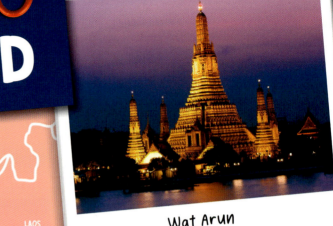

Wat Arun
BANGKOK

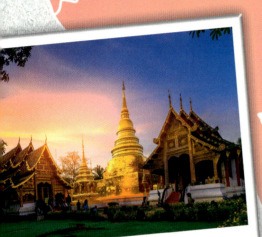

Wat Phra That Doi Suthep
CHIANG MAI

MYANMAR

LAOS

• Chiang Mai

• Udon Thani

Khon Kaen

• Bangkok

Pattaya

CAMBODIA

VIETNAM

Phuket

Hat Yai

Railay Beach
KRABI PROVINCE

Thailand is a popular tourist destination. People visit the country to see the incredible sites, eat amazing food, and meet the friendly locals.

MALAYSIA

Wat Chaiwatthanaram
AYUTTHAYA

Khao Yai National Park
NAKHON NAYOK PROVINCE

Rama IX Park
BANGKOK

SNAPSHOT

COUNTRY

Kingdom of Thailand

CAPITAL | **OFFICIAL LANGUAGE**

Bangkok | Thai

AREA | **POPULATION**

513,120 square kilometres | 70,015,456 (2021)

HIGHEST POINT Doi Inthanon, 2,565 metres

RELIGIONS Buddhism (majority)

CURRENCY | ฿ Thai Baht

GOVERNMENT | Constitutional Monarchy with a Parliamentary system of Government

WELCOME TO THAILAND

Buddhism is very important in Thailand and the Thai elephant is considered sacred

The Kingdom of Thailand is in Southeast Asia, bordered by Myanmar and Laos to the north, Cambodia to the east and Malaysia to the south. Thailand borders the Gulf of Thailand to the south and east, and the Andaman Sea to the west. People began living in the area around 7,000 BC. Formerly known as Siam, it was renamed Thailand in 1939. Thailand is a constitutional monarchy and a parliamentary democracy. It has a Prime Minister and the King is Head of State.

Major Industries

Thailand's major industries include tourism, textiles and the manufacturing of footwear, furniture, electronics and automobile parts.

Thailand is the world's second largest exporter of rice

Tourism is a major contributor to Thailand's economy

Main Agriculture

Thailand's main agriculture includes rice, rubber, sugarcane, corn, cotton and soyabean.

Some Kayan Lawhi of the Karen hill tribe wear brass coils to extend their necks

People

Thailand has a population of over 70 million people. All citizens are called Thai, however there are various groups within the population. Ethnic Thai make up about 90 per cent of the overall population. Chinese settlers make up about 10 per cent. There are smaller populations of Malays and refugees from Myanmar, Laos and Vietnam. The Thai are predominantly Theravada Buddhist, influenced by a mix of traditional rituals.

Hill Tribes

There are many indigenous groups in Thailand. They are known as hill tribes. Each hill tribe has its own customs, language, dress and spiritual beliefs. Some of the hill tribes include:

- Hmong
- Akha
- Karen
- Mien

Hmong children in traditional dress

Sea Nomads

The Moklen, Moken and Urak Lawoi are three groups that are collectively known as sea gypsies. They live in huts on the water off the Andaman coast.

Moken villages are built on stilts along the shoreline

Tourism is a major contributor to Thailand's economy, with an average of 40 million visitors annually. There is so much to see and do in 'The Land of Smiles.' From stunning beaches and island hopping, to visiting northern hill tribes and ancient ruins, it is no wonder that Thailand is such a popular destination.

TOP SITES

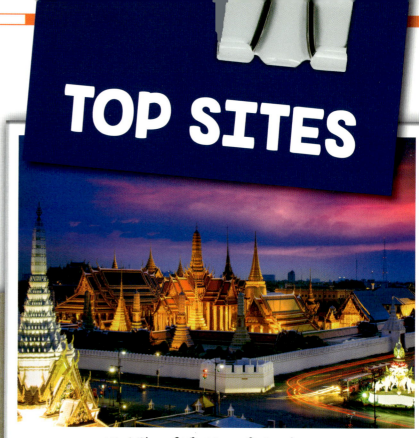

Wat Phra Si Rattana Satsadaram is the most sacred temple in Thailand

GRAND PALACE, BANGKOK

Chiang Mai

Chiang Mai was founded in 1296 as the capital of the ancient Lanna Kingdom. Today, it is Thailand's northern capital and one of its most popular destinations. People visit Chiang Mai for the cooler climate, the great food and as a starting point to explore some of the nearby hill tribes. The many ethnic minorities who live in the area around Chiang Mai have preserved much of their traditional customs, beliefs and traditions.

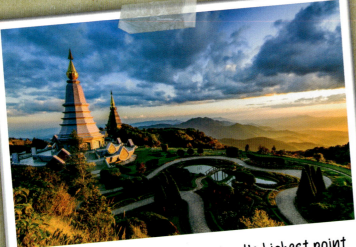

Doi Inthanon Mountain is Thailand's highest point

CHIANG MAI

Bangkok

Thailand's capital is a modern mega-city with a historic heart. The Chao Phraya River is filled with boats ferrying people to and from many of the city's major sites. The banks are teeming with life, from precariously built slums to the opulent Grand Palace. Weaving off the river are countless canals, known as klongs. Until a few decades ago they were so crowded with boats that policeman were used to direct traffic.

Ayutthaya

In 1350, the city of Ayutthaya was founded and a monarchy was established. It was the capital of Siam for 400 years. Today, Ayutthaya Historical Park contains ruins of the royal palace and numerous temples. Ayutthaya is one of Thailand's most important archaeological and tourism sites.

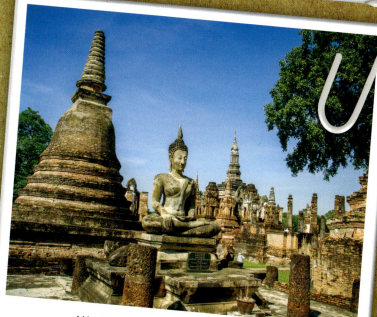

Wat Mahathat Buddhist temple
AYUTTHAYA

The Kaeng Krachan Forest complex was inscribed in the UNESCO World Heritage List in 2021

Important Sites

As of 2021, there are six UNESCO World Heritage sites in Thailand, which make up the country's most important tourist destinations. There are three World Cultural Heritage Sites and three World Natural Heritage Sites.

Fast Fact

Bangkok's full ceremonial name is Krungthepmahanakhon Amonrattanakosin Mahintharayutthaya Mahadilokphop Noppharatratchathaniburirom Udomratchaniwetmahasathan Amonphimanawatansathit Sakkathattiyawitsanukamprasit.

Different generations in Thai families often live and work together

Family is very important in Thailand and many people live in multi-generational homes. Care of the young or elderly family members is provided by other adults at home, who also work either in or away from the home.

Health

Thailand has a high standard of free, universal health care. There are over 1,000 public hospitals and almost 400 private clinics. Vaccinations have reduced the occurrence of diseases like cholera, tuberculosis, smallpox and tetanus. Chemical sprays have reduced the instance of malaria by reducing the mosquito population.

In Thailand, many children receive their vaccinations at school

EDUCATION

Education is compulsory in Thailand and all children attend primary school between the ages of six and eleven, followed by three years in lower secondary school. After that, students may continue to upper secondary school for another three years, before applying for one of the country's many universities. Teachers are highly respected in Thailand and each school year begins with a Wai Kru ceremony where students honour their teachers.

Almost one million Thai children attend small rural schools

Upper secondary school is important if students want to go on to university

Thai students honour Teacher's Day each January with Wai Kru ceremonies

NATIONAL DRESS

chut Thai Chakkri is a very popular national dress style

When Thailand's Queen Sirikit went to Europe and the United States in 1960, she had eight official outfits. These later became accepted as part of Thailand's national dress, called chut Thai.

Popular chut Thai include:

- Ruean Ton
- Chitlada
- Amarin
- Borom Bhiman
- Chakkri
- Dusit
- Chakkraphat
- Siwalai

Queen Sirikit (left), during the Royal visit to Europe in 1960

chut Thai Chitlada is a ceremonial outfit for the daytime

LANGUAGE

Thai is a tonal language. There are five tones for each word and each different tone changes the meaning of the word. For example, the word mai can mean 'wood', 'silk', 'new', 'burn' or 'not', depending on what tone is used to pronounce it.

Thai has 20 consonants, written with 43 different symbols. This means that many symbols are pronounced the same. It has 14 long vowel symbols, and 18 short ones.

Learn the Lingo: Thai

Females end sentences with the word ká/kâ. Males end sentences with the word kráp.

Sawadee (kráp/ká/kâ)
Hello

Sa bai dee mai (kráp/ká/kâ)
How are you?

Khob khun (kráp/ká/kâ)
Thank you

La gorn (kráp/ká/kâ)
Goodbye

Aaj ja (kráp/ká/kâ)
Maybe

khor thoad (kráp/ká/kâ)
Sorry/excuse me

Aroy (kráp/ká/kâ)
Delicious

Mai (kráp/ká/kâ)
No

LIFE IN CITIES

Over 50 per cent of Thailand's population live in cites and urban areas close to work. Urban residential areas include homes such as apartments, condominiums and town houses.

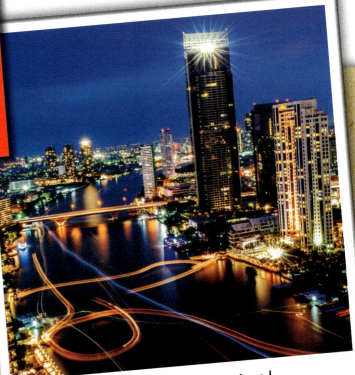

Bangkok is the largest and most developed city in Thailand

The largest city is the capital, Bangkok, with an estimated 11 million inhabitants. Rapid population growth in Bangkok has outpaced town planning. This has led to traffic congestion, air pollution and strained infrastructure.

Bangkok's streets can be very congested

Traffic can be chaotic in Thailand's cities. Bus travel is the most popular long distance method of travel, while scooters and motorbikes are the preferred method for shorter distances.

About 50 per cent of Thailand's population lives in rural areas. Their way of life has not changed much for generations. Families live in traditional style homes and own farms or small businesses. Many generations live under one roof.

LIFE IN RURAL AREAS

Sloping hillsides are terraced to allow farming of stepped rice fields

Most Thai villages are small. The residents are farmers or, in coastal areas, they fish. Villagers have about one acre of land where they have gardens and orchards. Crops like rice, sugarcane, potatoes and rubber trees are usually farmed on land just outside the village. Most villages only have a few stores, basic public services and a small school. The Buddhist temple is at the centre of life for most villagers.

Rice plants don't need water, but the flooded beds keep pests and weeds away

Each November, at the end of the agricultural season, many farmers head to the cities to look for temporary work before returning to their villages for the planting season in April.

Buddhists sit on the floor to pray, barefoot and facing a statue of Buddha

The majority of Thais are Buddhists, although other religions practiced include Christianity, Hinduism, Sikhism and Islam.

Buddhism

Around 95 per cent of Thailand's population is Buddhist with the vast majority practicing Theravada Buddhism. Many young Thai men become monks for a period of time.

Buddhists live by these five Moral Precepts:

- Do not harm any living thing
- Do not take what is not given
- Do not engage in sexual misconduct
- Do not lie or gossip
- Do not consume intoxicating substances

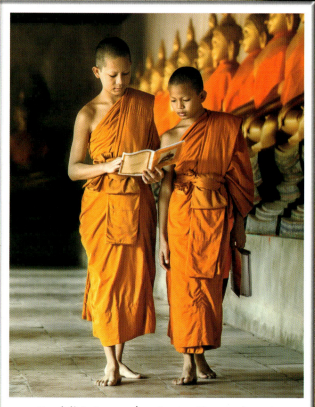

Buddhist monks train throughout their childhood before they can be ordained at the age of 20

Fortune-telling

Many Thai people consult fortune-tellers and palmists. In Siam, astrologers were consulted before a major battle. Today, astrologers are often consulted before making decisions about marriage or business, and even to help choose auspicious days for major events.

Thai families often consult fortune tellers before making important decisions

Islam

Approximately four per cent of Thailand's population is Muslim. The majority can be found in the southern provinces, near Malaysia.

Songkhla central Mosque in Yat Hai has an open prayer hall so lake-cooled air can circulate

Fast Fact

While citizens of Thailand are free to practice whatever religion they choose, or none at all, the King is constitutionally required to be a Buddhist as he is the Defender of the Faith.

Christianity

About a third of Thailand's minority peoples have converted to Christianity, but over all only one per cent of the population is Christian.

A LAND OF TEMPLES

There are over 40,000 Buddhist temples in Thailand, official and otherwise. Thai temple architecture generally comprises of numerous buildings and the roofs have multiple tiers and gables ending in long, thin ornaments called chofahs.

The most important temple in Thailand is Wat Phra Si Rattana Satsadaram within the precincts of the Grand Palace in Bangkok. It is home to the sacred Emerald Buddha, carved from a single piece of jade.

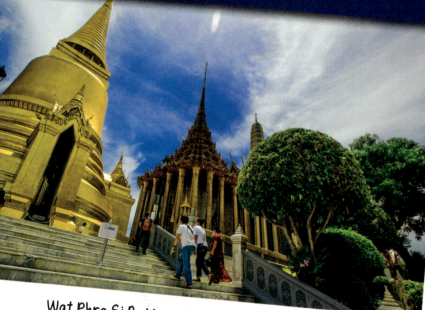

Wat Phra Si Rattana Satsadaram in Bangkok is the most sacred temple in Thailand

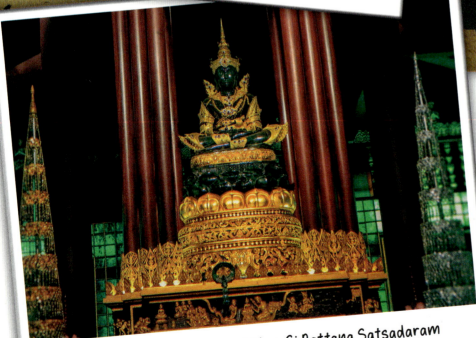

Emerald Buddha statue, Wat Phra Si Rattana Satsadaram
BANGKOK

One of the most famous temples is Wat Phra That Lampang Luang in northern Thailand. Dating from 1476, it is believed to be the oldest wooden building in the country. It is a great example of Lanna period religious architecture.

Wat Pho is one of Bangkok's oldest temples and one of six temples in the country classified as a first-class royal temple. It is famous for its 46-metre long reclining Buddha.

FOOD

Thai food is all about achieving perfect harmony between sweet, sour, hot and salty. The cuisine incorporates fresh vegetables and tropical fruits, seafood, meats and spices. Chilli is an important ingredient, as are garlic, ginger, fish paste, palm sugar, lemongrass, lime juice, coconut and soy sauce. Staples are rice, tofu, fish, pork and chicken.

Dishes vary around the country and there are regional influences. Central Thailand is heavily influenced by Royal Thai cuisine.

Pad Thai noodle with tofu and mixed vegetables

Thailand's National Dish

Thailand's national dish is also its most famous: Pad Thai. It consists of stir-fried rice noodles, vegetables, bean sprouts, peanuts, and egg. Meat or tofu versions are available. Originally it came from China, but Pad China doesn't have the same ring to it.

Every Meal is a Celebration

Large groups of family and friends don't need a reason to share a meal. Thai people believe food is a celebration and meant to be shared.

Massaman curry

Tom yum goong

Miang Kham, a snack often sold as street food

Royal Thai Cuisine

Royal Thai Cuisine originated in the ancient capital of Ayutthaya in 1351, with the recipes being served to the royal family since then. The focus is on seasonal produce and complex, delicate flavours. Everything on the plate must be edible, so no fish bones. Presentation is important and the dishes are exquisitely styled. Today, Royal Thai cuisine is enjoyed in restaurants all over the world.

Some of the better-known dishes are:

- Ranchuan curry
- Nam phrik long rue
- Massaman curry
- Fish cakes
- Tom yum goong

Street Food

Thailand's street food and night markets are world-renowned. There is always a delicious meal to grab outdoors. Street vendors cook quick meals on the spot.

LANDSCAPE

Doi Inthanon National Park in Northern Thailand is mountainous with temperate forests

Thailand is located in the heart of Southeast Asia and shares borders with Cambodia, Laos, Myanmar and Malaysia. It is a country with abundant natural resources and a wide variety of fauna and flora. Approximately 20 per cent of the country is mountainous. There are over 100 national parks, including more than 20 marine parks. It has four main regions, in the north, the northeast, the south and the central plains. Thailand's regions are divided into 76 provinces with the same names as their respective capitals.

North

The North is made up of temperate forests and mountain ranges that include the highest peak, Doi Inthanon. The Doi Inthanon National Park in Chiang Mai covers 482 square kilometres and is known as the 'Roof of Thailand'.

Central Plains

The fertile central plains are the centre of culture and business. The region is dominated by the Chao Phraya River, which runs for 372 kilometres, before draining into a delta south of Bangkok.

The Chao Phraya River runs through the mega-city of Bangkok

The Khorat Plateau is a farming tableland that floods during monsoon season

Northeast

The Khorat Plateau is a region of rolling low hills and small, shallow lakes and savannahs that drain into the Mekong River system. It regularly floods in the rainy season, but is otherwise hot and dry.

South

The mountainous south joins with the Malay peninsular. It is a region of mangrove rainforests and beaches, with beautiful islands off both sides of the peninsula. Some of Thailand's most famous islands include:

- Koh Phi Phi
- Koh Lanta
- Koh Samui
- Similan Islands

Koh Phi Phi is a popular tourist destination

Check it Out

Thailand is shaped like the head of an elephant. Can you see the elephant's head on a map?

Thailand's tropical climate is characterised by high temperatures and humidity throughout the year. April and May feature the hottest temperatures while the weather in June sees the monsoon pattern bringing heavy rain through to October. The climate varies by region, with cooler temperatures in the mountains in the north.

Monsoon rains often flood the streets in urban areas

Traditional houses

Traditional rural homes are made of wood, although palm thatch is also used in rural areas. The houses are lifted above the ground on stilts. This lifts the home above any flooding and lets air circulate when it is humid.

In many of the older houses there is no indoor plumbing so some homes don't have showers. The traditional way of showering is to throw water on your body. Shoes are removed at the door and most Thai homes display a photo of the King.

Local people who lost their homes in the tsunami gathered at a shelter in Takua Pa

Stranded ships remind visitors of the 2004 Tsunami and the 1,000s who died in the village of Ban Nam Khem

Natural disasters

The most common natural disasters to affect Thailand are floods and droughts. However, on December 26, 2004 a massive earthquake occurred under the Indian Ocean, triggering a devastating tsunami that killed over 230,000 people.

พื้นที่เสี่ยงภัยคลื่นยักษ์
TSUNAMI HAZARD ZONE

IN CASE OF EARTHQUAKE, GO TO HIGH GROUND OR INLAND

เมื่อเกิดแผ่นดินไหว ให้หนีห่าง
จากชายหาดและขึ้นที่สูงโดยเร็ว

Tsunami memorial in Phuket

Governments and organisations from around the globe sent relief workers to assist in the aftermath of this disaster. Since 2006, the Indian Ocean Tsunami Warning System has been in place.

FABULOUS FLORA & FAUNA

Flora

Thailand is well-known for its rich variety of flora and fauna. The country has more than 27,000 flowering species, including gardenias and hibiscus. There are over 1,300 types of orchids. Banana, mango and coconut trees are just some of the many tropical trees that flourish there.

Hibiscus rosa sinensis, Bangkok

Bamboo is a quick growing plant that can be farmed for many purposes such as construction, handicrafts and papermaking. There are sixty species of bamboo in Thailand.

Bamboo is used is weave sunhats

Patara Elephant Farm, Chiang Mai

Fauna

Thailand is famous for its elephants, although very few Asian elephants remain in the wild. Elephants can still be found giving rides to tourists, but there are more elephant sanctuaries being built where tourists can come into contact with these creatures under more humane conditions.

Thailand has about 300 mammal species, some of which are listed as vulnerable or critically endangered. About ten per cent of the world's bird species are in Thailand, as well as many unique amphibians, reptiles and insects.

Some of Thailand's unusual animals include:

- Siamese cat
- Bumblebee bat
- Clouded leopard
- Irrawaddy dolphin
- Siamang
- Sambar deer
- Sun bear
- Water buffalo

Siamang

Sambar deer

THE ARTS

Thailand has a rich history of traditional arts. Modern arts such as cinema, literature and music are enjoyed, as well as traditional arts that are hundreds of years old.

Khon is a traditional Thai masked dance drama performance

Depiction of the Ramayana story in Bangkok's Grand Palace

Literature

Thailand has a long oral tradition. Stories about the king and his court were told at festivals and gatherings long before they were ever written down. The best know story in Thailand is the *Ramakien* (The Glory of Rama), which is based on the Indian Hindu story, Ramayana. Over the years this story has been told in books, puppet shows, and other art works.

Ceramics

Ceramics have been made in Thailand for thousands of years. Pale green stoneware called celadon is the most refined of all the ceramics. Pottery and statues are still crafted today.

Weaving

Some of the world's most beautiful fabric comes from Thailand. The country is famous for its Thai silk.

cotton yarn is woven into fabric

Umbrellas

In Chiang Mai province there is a town called Bo Sang that has been making umbrellas for over 100 years. These handcrafted umbrellas are made from cloth stretched over bamboo, or from paper produced from the bark of the mulberry tree. They are painted with bright colours, often with floral patterns.

FLAG, SYMBOLS AND EMBLEMS

Flag of Thailand

The Thai flag has five horizontal stripes. The red stripes symbolise the blood of life, the white stand for the purity of the Buddhist faith and the blue represent the monarchy. The design was officially adopted on September 28, 1917.

National Emblem

The National Emblem is the Garuda, the mythical half-man half-bird. It is used on government and royal seals.

National Anthem

Phleng Chat Thai is the Thai National Anthem and it is played twice a day in schools, offices, factories and government buildings.

National Symbol
Elephant

GLOSSARY

Lotus flowers are grown for sale to tourists at floating markets

Buddhism religion based on the teachings of Buddha

culture practices, beliefs and customs of a society or people

dialect variation of a language unique to a region

endangered species at risk

ethnic group of people who share a common culture, language and heritage

monarch king or queen

monsoon season of heavy rain

plateau large, flat area found in higher regions

Thailand's Yee Peng festival is celebrated on the full moon of the 12th lunar month of the year

Siam the former name of Thailand

sustainability supporting the environment

tropical hot, humid climate

Tsunami destructive surge of ocean water

INDEX

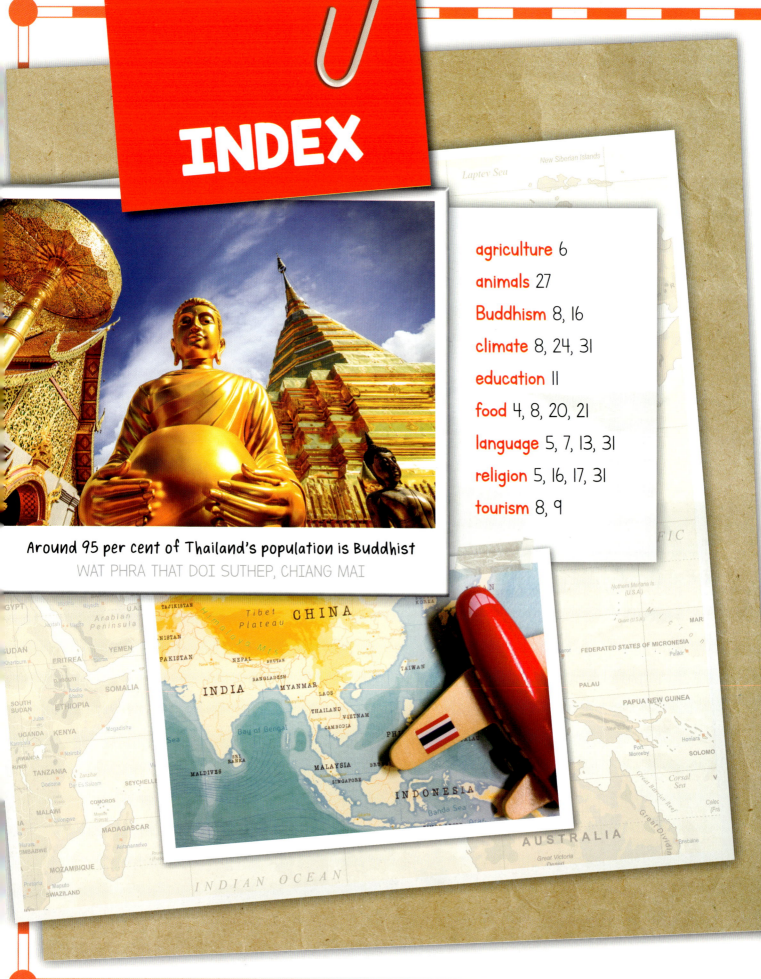

Around 95 per cent of Thailand's population is Buddhist

WAT PHRA THAT DOI SUTHEP, CHIANG MAI

agriculture 6

animals 27

Buddhism 8, 16

climate 8, 24, 31

education 11

food 4, 8, 20, 21

language 5, 7, 13, 31

religion 5, 16, 17, 31

tourism 8, 9

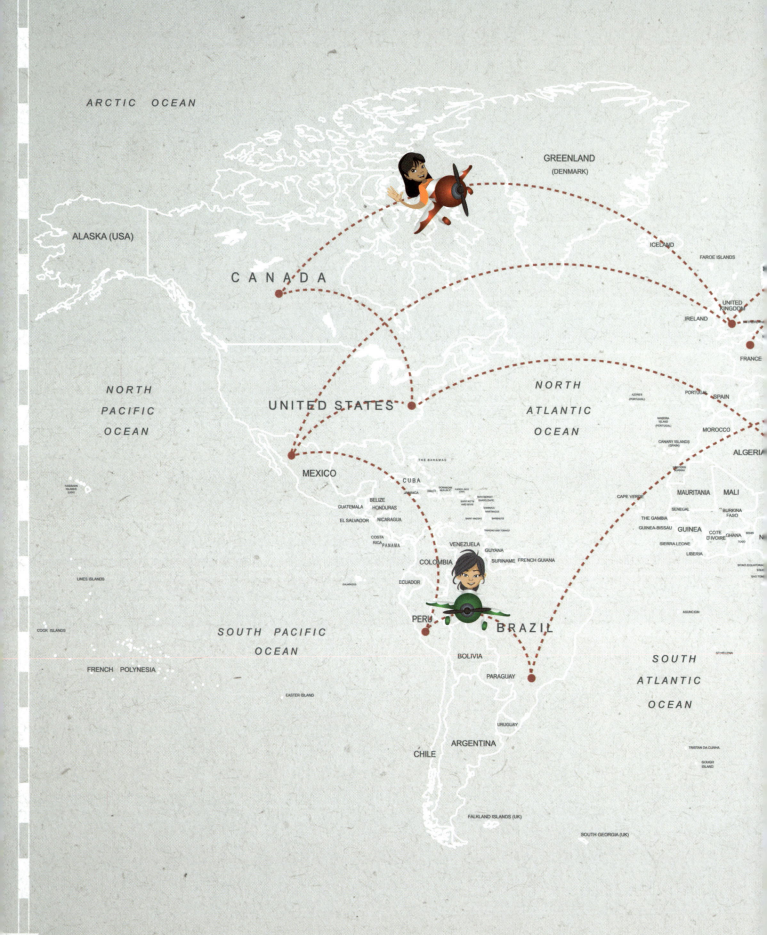